Objects in Motion

Jonathan Katz

C&R Press
Conscious & Responsible

First Edition
1 2 3 4 5 6 7 8 9

Selections of up to one page may be reproduced without permission. To repro-
duce more than one page of any one portion of this book, write to publishers
John Gosslee and Andrew Sullivan.

Cover art and design: Rachel Kelli
Interior design by Ali Chica

Copyright ©2018 Jonathan Katz
Library of Congress Cataloging-in-Publication Data

ISBN: 978-1-936196-93-7
Library of Congress Control Number: 2018956122

C&R Press
Conscious & Responsible
crpress.org

For special discounted bulk purchases, please contact:
C&R Press sales@crpress.oorg
Contact info@rpress.org to book events, readings and author signings.

For Terri and Jessica

Table of Contents

Objects in Motion

Journeyman

Acknowledgment

"Box Jelly" has appeared previously in REUNION/The Dallas Review, Vol. 7.

Objects in Motion

Your Preface

How poor a language clears no pathway
to disheveled beauty, for the dank and tussled hair
of intimacy lacks a phrase, begs a word
for unadorned and unkempt faces glimpsed
in waking blinks by lovers who have lain
beside each other quietly for not so many hours
as they could properly call rest?
Perhaps one word for that first sight
in dawn, another in full sunlight,
and a third in shadow overcast.

Shouldn't there be a word for lovers parting,
for reluctance that recalls a pleasure
so intense no measure of a time or distance
has the meaning now it had before,
for longing mixed with emptiness?

What if this fevered tongue had no vocabulary
to express anticipation thorned with trepidation,
fear of showing what I lack without you,
how it all seems incomplete, and either
you find that pathetic or repulsive,
or esteem it sweet? That is why I crave the word
that sets me up as more like brave
than ravenous, and us more like fulfillment
of an aspiration, of a destiny, than a plea.

Reader, you must add a preface to all dictionaries
that reminds us what an inarticulate,
sad and needy species we would be
if all we had were pages that confirmed
agreement on the easy aspects of our history

without a trope for freefall and the swoop up
of the fledgling from the nest, without the image
of a finger tracing longingly the rare bird flying west,
without a lexicon of poetry.

Songs and Seasons

What brought the kindred spider to that height,
Then steered the white moth thither in the night?

- Robert Frost

Ephemeroptera

What I liked most about singing Fre-re Jac-ques
was the actual sound of the bells
Din Din Don   Din Din Don
and I was pleasantly misled by
Dor-mez – vous?   Dor-mez – vous?
to think of that as a quiet inquiry
instead of an insistent Hey you! Get up!
So years later my expectation of a dormitory
was a comfortable sleeping place
decorated with curtains and pillows and not
the Spartan academic version of a pillbox
so cramped we members of the climbing club
could easily traverse the room 3 feet above the floor
which we did and only broke one reading lamp
before engaging in far riskier behavior.
As I said, the distances were not far,
we were young, so there you go.
And now we're pleasantly engaged enough to grapple
with the reason we are here today: what dormancy is,
what the point is of the mayfly life we lead,
the insect version being only minutes, maybe hours.
Breathing air since crawling underwater for a year
they up and swarm, they hover, mate in flight and die.
Imagine if you had just seconds to inhale everything.
A trillion flapping Tiffany-window-winged corpses
glisten gloriously on the water. In the world
of fish food there is none more bounteous or beautiful
and the ending or beginning is the eggs descending.
In the model of our individual conscious lives book-ended
by eternity, that is our world, too, so soaring and so brief.
The endless dormant portions when we are immersed communally
befuddle us with how much of existence they fill up.

We architects envision boundless pain, celestial pleasure,
void or some molecular collective soup. We song
writers grow big eyes and strong appendages to grasp
each other close as flies investing all their currency
of time to learn what ecstasies there are to share
this time around and how these can be cashed right now,
forever being short or long depending
and then *Din Din Don   Din Din*

Poem not a Poem

Mountains separate me and a man, and link us:
our falling hair makes us foresters in our ways.
Tree lines calibrate our passing years as if stone grew.

The servant of these processes is not without their power;
rocks furtively align themselves between us as I write,
with movements like the lengthening of stalks
above potatoes' earthbound eyes.

This man sits at his desk, he might be reading,
branches scratching at the window muffled by the wind;
just beyond the sill, pebbles dropped from beaks of birds
might spread their magic circles in the pond
and he might not look up, no more
than sunflowers at midnight search the sky.
He counts, as I, the many ways weeds overgrow a garden,
each subtle as the winter and her petal glazed in ice.

It seems an equal charm that keeps a window safe from branches;
one might even hear the wind that carries everything
that ever was or yet may be before it,
all the rocks outside might be alive and dancing,
yet one might sit and read. At last
the swallow seeks the south, snow falls,
the mole in his solid sleep is as good
as a stone, as cold and still in the earth.

Has anyone ever known a song as powerful as the season?
A flower now would be a dream, a poem.

April

The black fruit flies emerge
from the dark drain pipe into the blinding bathroom,
where I await, the supreme hunting species,
swatter in hand, murder in eye,
pathetic guilt in afterthought
because their two lace wings in flight
shape a heart whose rapid, random beat
is doomed, as the cow,
whose life—and death—are longer,
as the mink, who gets to play a bit
and beg the question, as the sprung gazelle,
whose exquisite rainbow arc is intersected
by the cheetah at its contact point with earth.
So here is a poem of pleasure and pain,
of past and present and never again,
the issue of balance and worth.

To me, April coming as cruel rang false.
Lack of April seemed bleaker, a sere field,
and winter worse, the days of April gone
like holes in a thin, cloth coat through which
the wind in its volley of frigid needles
announces the imminent snow.

But maybe it's just a matter of perspective.
In April, all aswarm with fear of loss,
I remember looking down at you.
It was when you last lay your head
on my white pillow, how your eyes
that moment closed – then opened wide,
and I could see my face reflected,
lonesome lotus bud in each dark pond.

A single fly-wing-flutter later,
I was stung by how the season had unfurled
its flag of rampant ferment, floods and insects,
and had staked it in the flowering world;
your hair flowed out and settled
like a silken pool of blood,
and, mindful that I could have chosen
between nothing and that stinging resurrection,
I surrendered to the Spring.

Envy of Robert Hass's Poem

> And   the   mute   women   …   seeing
> The awful longing in his eyes, are changed forever
> On their rocky waste of island by their imagination
> Of his imagination of the song they didn't sing.

>   — from "Envy of Other People's Poems," Robert Hass

The amorous nymph, Calypso, swore to the captain of her oar
the lonely Greek king stranded on her island confessed the following:
The sirens kept the distance that was part of their allure
and kept their silence as bold bound libertine Odysseus strained
against his knotted ropes, his singing unsuccessfully
drowned out by waves and winds that washed the cliff-walled shore
and splashed against the rocks on which the sirens lay;
the hull boards creaked, the sails filled and preened away
from the stubborn mast like lusty swans swimming in the air;
it was he, Odysseus, whose song was lost at sea,
whose strong voice failed, who wept his hot, frustrated tears,
their infinitesimal warmth whirled awash in the deep salt churn,
the sirens hoping for a soaring sound like trumpets and thunder
from his throat, loud enough to scatter the storm-dark clouds,
then intone so fluid a melody, the white wound waters would unroll,
the sky clear, the golden chariot of the sun appear, the sirens glow,
their long siren hair loll about their slipper-shell siren ears,
and, bathed in the slow tidal syllables Odysseus would then sing,
all the blood and honey in their siren bodies would ebb and flow.

Why did the air and ocean conspire these thousands of years ago
to humiliate a hero, to drown out the earnest explorer's desire
when all of nature's beauties were spread out and open for him?
Why is it so important we be told how clever he became at things?
Would that he never had to sail on and learn how to be cunning,
that it all were simpler and there were less one has to know.
Would that it had been so and our world the stuff of siren imaginings.

Hostages

it's bad enough that logic makes us understand
I think therefore I am means nothing since
the I that thinks already is presumed
there is thought therefore I am would make
it meaningful except *that* therefore doesn't work
what really is sad is that truth
if what we mean by that word is veracity
could never equal beauty
unless logic per se is a fiction
which one might conclude given
the ticking clock trap of the breathing body

a bird flies in one kitchen window out another
that is life the element promethium so unstable
like Van Gogh it cannot live on Earth it is
detected in the spectrum of a star
in the constellation of Andromeda
poets and philosophers have at it
athlete aging or musician dying young
both true where lives their loveliness
is it in the photo of the violin unstrung
words on pages headstones
in the snowy fields we walk among
hostages of that crazed kiss timelessness
the lush and fragrant language of green spring
singing in our ears the sun exploding on our skin

To the Bus Driver

Allow me to introduce myself.
I am the man who stepped in front of the bus
that you were driving.
I had my reasons.
It is true you may have been distracted
by someone wearing a white cap
or a closely fitted jacket, tight slacks,
smoking a cigarette or walking a feisty puppy.
A beautiful melody may have seized your mind,
you may have suddenly remembered
the touch of warm fingers on your bare arm,
the slight movement of a head resting on your shoulder,
or the fertile smell of a lover's hair.
You may have been immersed
in a deep pool of introspection.
I apologize for welcoming you back this way,
but I had to take control of my direction
and this is the way I did it. Numbness
never was my chosen destination.
I embraced the hurtling moment,
leaned into it trying to remind myself of pleasure.
Maybe you won't forgive me and maybe you can't.
I pray you can forgive yourself for harm without intent.
If I could plant one thing I've learned within you,
I would say believe that life is rich and sweet,
redeemable as a tired field tilled with fresh manure,
seeded full of hope and harvested when time can do no more,
worth the work – and worth the fighting for.

Defining Irony

What they don't teach you is
that you can't live without it.
Without it, there is no context
outside of yourself
and whatever bothers you
flows out in all directions
to the horizon like a liquid
that keeps your toes and feet wet
all the time or a gas
that irritates your lungs,
your throat, your eyes.
The point is there is nowhere
to escape, but when the student
says I read Sylvia Plath because
then I feel less alone, there
you are; there you go.

Accounting

Once you are dead,
all the ones you ever called beloved
steal away to their secret offices,
turn on the naked light bulbs,
settle in their mahogany swivel-chairs,
open the roll-top desks,
slide out the bottom left-hand drawers
and lift out the heavy ledgers,
thumb through the green-lined pages
with the vertical red-lined column
until they find the right vacancy,
put on their dark visors
to shield their eyes from the harshness
that illuminates these work places,
touch their quills to their lips,
dip them into the black ink well
and center, in their best cursive script,
the letters of their private name for you
along the top of the uppermost line.

They list all the accounts and all the items in them.
They speed through the resolved,
linger nostalgically over the receivables,
and enumerate the payables, some with longing,
some with relief. In summing up, they learn
whether they hoped, all along, for a net payable,
for a debt they will never have to cover, or not.
And another lesson: giving more than receiving
turns out to be pretty much a matter
of circumstance and timing, which can be
disconcerting to a lover left behind.

Sometimes extending metaphor can be misleading;
to sort it out, the inside auditor must get involved.
It might appear the soul of the deceased is unaccounted for,
when it's just the opposite in fact,
because that singular commodity inhabits
each transaction passionately intact, each transaction
a little business that refuses to dissolve,
that lives on in all the columns –
receivable, payable and unresolved.

A Poem about Dancing

the block rests on the table top
a cube of soft wood with worn rounded corners
one piece of a child's Victorian or Edwardian set
the letter R in red ink stamped on one side
looks like a protruding stomach
supported by one straight leg
and one leg advancing tentatively
on another side the profiled head of a lady
high piled creamy brown hair in Gibson Girl swirls
that breathtaking side curl caressing her ear
around you go a side shows a rhinoceros
another offers a lily-of-the-valley
on top three stripes parallel painted blue
project up in slight relief from the surface
and there is an under side also could be cut
so maybe the other blocks were carved to interlock

a streak of sunlight falls across the table
but not across the block which sits outside it
above in the pond of illuminated air
dust motes float and drift

the window frames the trees' golden hour
dust also settles visibly and invisibly
a hundred and twenty years of dust settling
on the table and the block begins now
an earthquake of 6.2 on the Richter scale
begins now to shake the ground so far away
we think the wooden block does not respond
but if we had a lens and a scale fine enough
we could see the child's wooden block moved
and measure the fluctuations of its weight

Stichomancy

I'd never heard this word before
serendipity led me to it in a dictionary.
If your literary learning's fancy-shmancy,
you just might recognize that "mancy"
means to tell the future using something.
That something in this case is just a word,
one chosen randomly by opening a book
and pointing to the page, your finger
a divining rod, the future fluid as water.
This is how you might find "Banach space."
If you were I, you'd be relieved to have
your almost total ignorance of math erased
and in its place the knowledge that a mental athlete
was born in Krakow, who, before the age of fifty-three,
conceived "a vector space on which
a norm is defined that is complete."
You might wonder, as I do, what it was like
being born in 1892 and exiting the moment
both world wars had run their course,
the German plunder over, the Allied betrayals
of Poland at Tehran and Yalta *faits accomplis*,
and the graphs of a new planet plotted.

Envision the world before Descartes created
the x and y axes. It hardly seems that one
could chart a course of meaning in life,
the growth of a family's wealth over time,
the acreage of taxable fiefdom by battles,
the exponential increase of love required
on the top few inches of the earth's soil
as unfairness and grief blossom and colonize.

Now, our many axes can express both depth and time,
and the n-dimensional possibilities of all we can imagine.
Science fiction once considered merely odd becomes a prophecy
and best-selling non-fiction outlines the mind of God.
I don't pretend that stichomancy makes me gifted
with perspectives others can't expect to see; in fact,
it's blinded me to know how universally and at random
all the crow-like facts converge like minions on a tree,
and how like witchery with purpose that can seem to be.
One doesn't need a theory of everything to understand
how any life that ends at any age can be described
as neat, as lifted to the cusp of making sense,
as product of a winding line through history
of sometimes straight and sometimes curved trajectory,
as ending where it had to, just as if a finger
had descended with authority from out of sight
to indicate the final grains of sand had sifted
to the bottom of the glass, to mark upon the graph
the fatal point at hand, and simultaneously to command
that all coordinates be shifted.

The Center

"We plan on signing a center for the coming season and will
pay you $110.00 per game if you wish to join the 'Packers'."

— Green Bay Football Corporation to Gerald Ford
February 11, 1935

President Gerald R. Ford, Jr., granted an interview
to historian Michael Beschloss, the sole price
silence while the only unelected holder of his office
lived. Now he moves in death's fixed orbit
and we receive the stony news of how he would
have handled this and that decision differently
than others, just one instance being his insistence
that the Shah could have been pushed along
reform's path by a more adept American, by him.
Imagine, moderation as a credo
of our latest nuclear companion; imagine,
no incendiary threats from either side;
imagine no embargo, just imagine,

and imagine, how incredulous his academic
interviewer was when Milton, asked why *Paradise
Lost* depicted earth as focus of the solar system
a hundred years since Galileo taught us otherwise,
responded, Because that makes no difference.
All the motions of the universe, no matter
how erratic, no matter where we enter
or where we stand, can be plotted;
from eternity's perspective, every moving point—
a little piece of fruit denied, an acquiescence
to a bride, a step too far, or reticence
when just a little spine is called for, or, when
reticence would better serve, a momentary pride,

a lazy voter here and there and multiplied—
each and every moving point a human occupies
can scramble all the maps of heaven,
scatter, fling and bring down angels,
render in the almost infinite ballot box
of almost unrelated votes a loser or a winner;
beware, the star whose chariot your mentor rides
may fall and, suddenly, your modest light
ignites and all that churns and glimmers
circles round and you become: the Center.

Penknife

When you lose a poem, you can hardly believe it;
the pad of yellow-lined paper was right there on the desk.
Your mate thinks maybe you were drunk or sleepily imagining;
the cleaning lady does not get what you are saying:
Was it like a newspaper? Was it luggage? How big?
Sometimes you can only remember the topic.
It was about my father's farts—yes, of course
it was funny, but it was serious, too,
like farts are, before they are wafted away,
and had charm and personality, like farts do.
Okay, I can't explain it now, but it was really
going to be good; and sometimes
you can only recapture a line:
"And the comet returned, like a bee
lade with frozen pollen, having merely
traversed the universe, to the dark petals
patiently waiting." In that poem, I know
that the comet was somehow my heart,
I just don't remember how, and then
that scrap I scribbled on slipped away.
Disappearances must take place at a moment,
though your realization might be gradual
or long after the fact. If there's purpose to them,
it is certainly hidden to you;
someone needed the part of the page
you left empty for grocery listing,
or, when they saw the silverfish,
the nearest thing was your pad—end of story,
and that lack of meaning is better, right? —
wouldn't it be a crueler world if fragments of poems
did vanish on purpose, if people we once loved
moved purposefully out of our lives instead of

forgetting to call on our birthday, our sexual
images fading from recall like old photos used to
from overexposure to light. Still, at night, I imagine
the finding of poems, the joys and the binding
together through sorrows their narrative lines
and their lyrical rises and falls would describe;
how, like the kitten that just wandered off,
or, like that attractive stranger on the bus,
yes, even like those we've lived with drifted now away,
those drafts we lost found their way back,
not as single works with a history that happened,
but as anthologies, compendia of all the possibilities
for stories starring us and various starlets.
I am amazed at all the ways I could be satisfied
that whittled down to one,
at all the literature stillborn in notes to self,
how great is our capacity to love in retrospect
and at a distance all the choices
that we didn't care to make, or didn't even notice
while artifacts in process vanished constantly and
while the penknife of our million indecisions
carved the sculpture of the life we needed.

Hoarding

so we were talking about a friend of ours
next thing I knew we were talking about me
and the term hoarding was used and OK
so I got a little defensive but you know me
I started thinking about it when no one
was around and now my ground is staked out
in a highly structured way so to speak
I have to start with some admissions
since the last thing of which I care to be accused
is being in denial even if the flaw is very minor
of the kind that many people have and I'll just
leave which those are to your imagination
I am sure you are aware of several
of yours and so you understand
where I am coming from or from
where I am coming which is a little
hoarding of correctness for which I
feel no apology is necessary

admission number one it's difficult to reach
the Chaucer essays while the *Dia de los Muertos*
beauty parlor and the billiard hall are on display
and easy access to *The Oxford English Dictionary*
is denied by those enchanting Nigerian fertility
carvings while the walls are blooming with Solomon
Islands frigate bird fish lures and cowrie and
bamboo sea current maps of the Marshalls
and masks such as the face made of a tortoise
carapace with dog-teeth for its mouth and so on to
admission numero dos the storage room garage halls
guest bedroom are like some novel social media
adorned with images and objects and sentinel statues

positioned to welcome and usher the curious along
who knit narrative threads pull together what they see
a theme here a logic there hint of a purposeful unity
driving my gathering of treasures and
admission three the travel section overflows
why should we not cruise Pest and Bratislava
not compare the drinks at dusk along the Danube
with those mixed at Riviera Caribbean and Hawaiian beaches
all of Homer is illuminated by the sun in Greece
I've heard how Northern Lights in Newfoundland change lives
and how the simplest tasks are beautiful in Bali
you could endlessly explore New Jersey talk about complexity
Pine Barrens farms and ranches diners yummy hot tomato pies
the Shore the regional museums tile and glass works
William Carlos Williams Ginsburg Springsteen
I have more admissions some I'm not yet ready to admit
but I think that I have demonstrated in denial
is not what I am

there are so many places yet to go
perceptions of creation how time never passes
where departed loved ones changed in subtle ways are
watching how we're doing they are hunting shopping
judging us as always pointing out the dangers
underneath the water's surface in the trees
the slithering and the prowling darkness
from the air they are collecting information
all the time on our behalf no one accuses
them of hoarding they are cousins of the people
everywhere who give their articles to thrift stores
where the diligent the mystified the hoping
not to be bewildered save and read and wonder
how their better ordered friends and family
make sense of troubling coincidences

where have they stored their base desires
about what are they most inquisitive
potentially impulsive how do they decide
when their rooms are filled up enough
with all the products of this mortal world

so that's the way it is my hopes are high
for mutually supportive companionship
as time goes by but listen babe and
buddies if I'm browsing and half-hidden
in the stationery pile is some dirty envelope
with large green unfamiliar postage
or some trinket struck by Claus of Innsbruck
comes my way I advise you let my epidemiology
play out I will make room on one shelf or another
in a drawer cabinet file hanging from
on next to or beneath whatever it's amazing
how this item juxtaposed with that becomes another
please come visit there is no end
to this variety of pleasure
I will have no rest
until you have seen everything

Millennium

For now he feard Eternal Death & uttermost Extinction
He builded Golgonooza on the Lake of Udan Adan
Upon the Limit of Translucence

- William Blake

Affluence

Around us lay a thick atmosphere
but it had proven to support life well
in our kind of country
and more dark years gathered
like particulate clouds steadily approaching
from far across the sea

We held our breath for love as if
for golden veins in endless cavern walls,
would strike lucky when our hope was almost lost,
would laugh to breathe that rich air once again,
then realize with what our lungs were full
as life here had become so dear and elsewhere cheap
that every joy was counterfeit

I tried to explain our affluence
and my cold kisses with a story:
when King Midas was a sleeping baby
ants carried grains of wheat to his lips
and great wealth was prophesied for his nation;
Orpheus, whose melodies made green trees and stones
dance into the shape of cities was his tutor;
all this before he ruled himself
the one just judge of music,
before his dream of all things gold
was granted by the gods
and he was gifted with the killing touch

That year we watched the drying leaves
gust dysrhythmic down the streets
until they piled themselves in heaps
against the walls of houses

like old coins falling from a great height
colliding with the earth and rolling uneven
to their abrupt metallic rest;
our hearts volcanic seemed a dream
like rivers beating against floodgates

The ground froze solid as the air was cold
and even when we kissed tonight
I thought of molten centers under pressure,
of tall trees dormant as the arctic night
and the tiny difference in the weather
or our constitution that determines
whether our seed will spring from one life to another
or will lie forever, decompose and be forgotten

American Disco

The most artful moment of the international
seminar was when the Serbian girl shin-kicked
the Turkish girl on the crowded dance floor.
From another angle, it might have looked accidental.
"What was that for?" I asked through a cloud
of American ignorance. "Five hundred years
of oppression," my explosive companion responded.
"Wow," I thought, "if people carried any more
ordnance of history they'd spontaneously combust
with a lot of collateral damage."
The next tune bouncing up was "Staying Alive."
My body felt lighter than the night air
and I glided away, my feet little detonators
wired to the power of the absence of history.

Part

What allegedly the Red Sea did was greeted differently
by the Children of Israel and the Pharaoh's army.
Differently greeted to this very day, though luckily
with pyramids, the Via Dolorosa, Yad Vashem,
so many ways to visit death and dying and hope
of resurrection layered on each other
thick as stacks of pungent flatbread,
all of us are interested in destination tourism.
Down the narrow alleys stories pile fine as phyllo
as they have since when the first salukis,
lured by lilting voices and the smell of roast gazelle,
loped within Sumerian gates and curled up by a fire.

A few days prior to the famous chase into the sea,
the first-born of Egyptians are said to have been slain,
the slaying said to be ordained, the tenth plague,
one last divine encyclical to set the slaves free.
"Children, too?" our good friend's daughter asks. "Yes."
"But what did they do?" "That is not the point,"
our good friend says. But in a way, it is the only.
The litigants divide, the governments and soldiers take a side,
comb them to the left or right, always innocents will die.
Where you're standing when the wall of water
does its thing will always make a difference.

Close up, story looks like a category of a larger history
but from a distance, history looks subservient to story,
generations learning scripts, taking roles to heart.
The method works. Rehearsing movements
makes the world a blocked-out stage,
the centuries and civilizations roll on by,
the surrounding scenery fluid on its rollers
powered from on high, so much so
it all seems just to flow.

The Art of War

> "Poets are the unacknowledged legislators of the world."
> —P. B. Shelley

Aeschylus gouged the eyes of Oedipus off-stage.
How crafty he intended that to be we'll never know.
Perhaps he thought that out of sight
the violence would terrorize us
not so much that we would have to turn away
and run from pity, that possible path to empathy.

How often are we in the room off-stage
from someone else's fall from greatness
or from adequacy, and, another way, how
many circumstances just the other side
of earshot or a wall could bring us down?
We could have been the only caring kin
so saddled with the parent's long and last
decline, we could have been the victim
of the innovation obsoleting our job,
our own beloved could have joined the military;
then we could be living what we can't even imagine.

Watch out for modern poets; they will bang pots all around
a phrase like "watch out." Once they say it,
they assume that you are looking as if from a tower;
they assume you have your time piece in your hand
as if it were a brooch, and if not that, a weapon.
"Unacknowledged legislators," that was centuries ago;
these expect like revolutionaries digital and rapid change;
they focus on the literal and its implications,
metaphorical applications, too, and heavy, heavy handed,

they proceed as if you have been personally warned,
there is no off-stage, there is no off-the-page,
this is not like Huxley's parrots caw "Attention"
from the island trees; these old and young are yelling
from the city, from the mountain, from the sand hill
"you are now alerted," they are arming IEDs,
you are right to be alarmed, since you are now responsible.

Box Jelly

sheer parachute of flesh
you sink and you float
canopied over the little sea
of your own juices
an unblinking eye
at each corner of your world
only hunger and a rare surprise
get a rise from you
adrift in an ocean
of imminent nourishment and death
you have mastered survival digesting
the smaller things who struggle more
while the idea of hope brews
outside your silent lethal territory
above and under and around
as trilobites come and go
and crabs grow legs and climb aground
for hundreds and hundreds of millions of years
the elegantly tentacled oration that you give
the rest of us who swim and crawl
through nature's dense curriculum
illustrates how buoyantly we too could live
without a tragic vision of it all

Hunting the Truth of Songs

Bring me my pumices, chalice and fice.
The great volcano spat these pieces for me
to tie hooks around and line together bobbing
in the bay for the fish waiting to nourish my family.
The grapes I crushed last year and prayed over
have turned to this heady juice transformed
like the crawler to the wings that fly and hover.
This cup is only roasted clay but fits my hand perfectly.
It holds enough to let me look around and laugh,
and so I think of it as fashioned by a shaman for a god.
My animal worships me as I the fire, water,
earth, air and all they offer up. It has no value
but a loyal spirit and so I love it like a son or daughter.

Our elders sing of meaty beasts asleep in cold caves
where white ocean foam floats down from the clouds
and lagoons grow a thick, dense skin hard as coconut.
If the hallowed songs are true, then there must be a liquid grace
connecting everything by sound and flow,
which magic my spirit might follow to walk
through the all-searing lava from the great volcano.
Measuring steps, hunting the truth of songs
in a molten world it is the fate of my tribe to go,
chanting, conjuring, shielded and shed of this body,
wishing the truth of words that fly in songs were easier to know.

Attractive Nuisance

Leave it to the lawyers to come up with phrases
that you can't flush out of mind. No wonder
Shakespeare has Dick the butcher and utopian
rebel say the first step is to kill them all;
the same reason, I think, that Plato urges
banishing all poets – inspiring language
becomes indistinguishable from power,
crowds out knowledge and becomes its own reality,
creates its solipsistic worlds that seem
to be driven by a plethora of fees and phonemes,
but really whirl without end in us deeper.
Madnesses, this meditation makes me realize,
are languages, and as such lure us in.
I have been so lonely that hearing voices offered company,
have been so powerless I gave commands to troops,
administrators, grocery clerks who were not there,
so disconnected to the day's events that I could see
how government officials, teachers, law enforcement
officers had conspired with random passersby
to disconnect me. *Prima facie* becomes *ipso facto*,
we are wired each to choose among the pretty
and utility madnesses continually. A lot of
small ones, misdemeanors, can be tolerated;
just beware the kind of tipsy where *habeas corpus*

and *duces tecum* are deployed by those you need
to maintain equilibrium. That's *pro bono*. All I ask
in recompense is let me pass and live among you.

Civilization

You insulted my team and threw me the finger.
So here's what I did.
When you ran into your house from your Subaru SUV,
arms full of groceries,
I noticed you didn't come back out
in the rain to lock it.
And when it got dark I crouched and slid
through the night like a ninja
and placed under the driver seat
a little bag of shit from my labradoodle
and drove out of the neighborhood
to stock up with another brand of bag
so if anyone asks me I can say
"I use these – they're great!"
And, so, eventually, maybe soon, you'll notice,
but there are rules,
even about questions you might ask,
and I could choose to be hurt or angry
and we'll both know what happened
and we'll both know that you deserved it
and maybe I'm the asshole here
but maybe not, because my labradoodle
has been trained well and has a sweet disposition
and there are pranksters everywhere,
and, bottom line: it's not polite,
not civilized, in my opinion,
to insult another guy's team.

Feeling Free

When I was a kid and my dad gave me a few bucks
to go into the city and have a good time and I got drunk with
my buddies and it didn't make any difference what I said
you know because my words were like big fuzzy glowing
Hawaiian lanterns strung from one place to another and
who cared they didn't mean anything I was feeling my oats
and harmless and if a girl wasn't pretty who cared what
she felt or thought I suppose if she had a good body
then maybe and we ate Chinese that night always liked
the clams black bean sauce was my style did some
dancing in a couple bars with music even danced
with one another stopped that straight away when
we saw in the mirror what that looked like knew
enough to stay away from colored neighborhoods
too dangerous with so many poor and what would
they want from the likes of us who knows but still
the best of all is knowing when you're schnockered
anything you say is OK and maybe you do really
"know more about ISIS than the generals" sure
if you believe it say so "the concept of global warming
was created by and for the Chinese" it's a hoax
by so-called scientists all around the world
no wonder all those coal those nuclear
those line assembly jobs are disappearing well if
that is your opinion you have got a right to your words
some percentage will agree no matter what
and I remember Ike denying that the U-2 Russia captured
was a spy plane everybody making up big numbers of the
North Vietnamese we'd killed when it was our own spirit dying
and how can anyone keep track what all the losers think those
drop outs soldiers who get captured refugees and immigrants
worshippers of weird religions ex-cons socialists – they're

atheists right I know they don't golf let's just all admit
that winning feels good you don't need alcohol at all
to get a high from winning you can always say
"and by the way Christianity will have power"
if I'm president no need to sacrifice a thing
words don't matter you know who you're meant to be
I remember how exceptional it feels to be free
to dip my tongue into the option to be incorrect politically
to drink up and go right ahead and take a little liberty

Turkey Thicket Park

Washington, DC, 1990

"Let's stick it to 'em, –"
and *he* called *me* that n-word.
I thought, "Yes, sir!"
and in that exalted moment you can bet
I kept my eyes more carefully on the ball
and, yes, I sure as hell did slash to the basket.
I looked around and it was true:
all of us were black and I
was just the only one with glasses.
Running back and forth all afternoon,
above the unforgiving surface of cement,
shining in my cleansing sweat and the irony of pride,
believing that the world is always young somewhere,
I glided over where the chalk and slate
and marl and sand had been mixed,
where shovels and wheel-barrows, jack-hammers and picks
had done the heavy lifting, but whether the lay of the land
could be fixed and leveled and last, only time would tell.

The M-Word

I was thinking about all the letters of the alphabet
that own words a person like me would never use
in a poem because we have certain social aspirations
and would like to be a First Lady's favorite poet some day
and I got to the m-word, right after the l-word
and just before the n-word (see what I mean?)
and I thought no no no no no unless since you could crawl
your relatives and friends showed you how to say that,
which mine did not (so I am f-worded in that regard),
but, like I say, I was thinking about the m-word
and how totally awesome it is to invoke
the presence of the person (not, presumably, the father)
who would trivially or malevolently or under false pretenses
overstep or abuse the most intimate physical relationship
with a woman who had given birth,
to be able to invoke that devilish or desiccated spirit
casually without feeling like you'd forgotten
to zip up your fly or like you just noticed a booger
hanging there after a whole night at a party,
and I'm thinking, that m-word doesn't just conjure up
that soul-sucker, it makes you wonder where the father is,
how the unholy threesome came to pass,
and I would think by containing in my mouth the vortex
of that obscene energy, I would declare
I can overcome any and all that is evil, unfair
circumstances, fight fire with fire, and in there is also,
don't you think, to sum up, a yearning for shelter,
that rock, that shield, that protector,
that end of day into bed tucker
with the power of an m-word come home,
seeking which we search the alphabet
for its infernal parlance, for sounds that

we can sprinkle like a spice to our taste,
that we can whisper, we can spit,
all the words that we can shout
to put the m-word hell flames out.

Millennium

At some point each of us sees the curve of the earth
as the top half of a smile, the lip of a world kissing heaven.
You cannot stand too close or details interpose:
genocide is much too big to understand. A severed
hand is not, a shot at night, the lonely child crying:
these suffice to make a ragged vista of the history
we prefer obscured by distance. The mystery is
still how little difference medicines have made
to treatment of our very basic malady, the one
we call humanity. The flea that caused the rats
to dance is mostly gone. The fly and the mosquito
have smaller chance to harm us than the tribe
made of our neighbors. Gods, crusaders and greedy
traders wield their charms with such immunity
as people choose to give them, and to lose
responsibility is quite the rage it was when
first we worshipped fire. No prophetic ire
kindled in a trance, no necromancer's cold gift
protected the terrain we now depart in search of
what will cure the human heart. All I know
of how to measure progress are the simplest tests:
at any time that new perspective bends horizons
and change of season tatters our fond habits,
if we say, and mean, we're all in on this journey,
that would be a step; and each time travelers realize
that but for the disguise of circumstance they could
have been each other, that would be another.
Whether tests like these are metaphors for kindness
or self-interest, there's no way to atone for what
we've done but to be different down the road,
or up the ladder. As each day ends its own
millennium, we're all together or alone—
a simple test for a simple truth, so life will matter.

Objects in Motion

Ontogeny recapitulates phylogeny.

- Ernst Haeckel

forever was never till now

- e. e. cummings

Objects in Motion

The barely perceptible hum I almost missed,
the tiniest oscillation on the screen,
was the dancing line of the first fireball returning.
Time as a tidal pool became clear,
how to stand quiet at its edge and look back in,
and later, looking back in, it became easy
to count every pulsar and nebula,
asteroid and comet, moon and meteor.
Not far from a field of corn on one planet,
next to a car parked beneath the pinball sky,
one person takes a small step forward
into the arms of another. I think,
from this distance, of their particulate image
rolling out in waves, riding the seahorse photons,
of the small step, of their arms enfolding,
of their stepping again and again into comforting arms,
the eternal momentum of objects in motion.

The Thing beyond Naming

(Labor Day weekend with the Lynch Family, 2014)

Let's tip a glass to the industry of physicists
as they smash the smallest articles of matter
searching for a string, a cloud, a wave, god-particle
sufficient to explain the stillness dance reveals,
the circumstance and movement that consecrate a universe with mass.

Let's call the feathery stitch that seams the sky and water:
osprey.
Let's call the porcelain path of gleam and shimmer in the bay:
the moon.
Exhaustedly, we all agree the adverbs ending music every evening are:
too soon.

We're magically included and befriended
with the eldest grand daughter and her intended;
this is the definition of how family is extended.

Our peccadilloes and our crushing woes
flow into the lines of blues we improvise
and nothing is as funny as the satire of ourselves.
Take heed, you scientists who seek a formula
for how a breaking world is mended.

The thing beyond naming
that happens to a place
inhabited by family;
let us call it: grace

The Penny

I found a penny on the ground outside the airport
just before I met you. Looking back,
I'm reminded now the Greeks believed
that each coin has a soul. That fact is from a short
sentence taken out of context, like conversation
in a taxicab. Couldn't say, for instance, whether
Lincoln's soul would be the one for every penny—
thoughtful, anguished, sturdy martyr.
All would be so similar, then, you
really couldn't say each had a soul.
Makes more sense to think the penny
takes its character from contact over time,
riding in the pocket of a person who likes
meeting people, passing from an agent
to a customer who trusts her, buying bread
for children growing up and soon away.
Then the penny would be really something,
presidential more than warm and pretty;
then you'd want to hold one that you found
and slow its circulation down a bit
until you understood just what it had accrued
inside that makes it precious.

My Sister

This poem turned out a lot shorter
than I had expected, like a path
through trees in the leafy time of year
when, with little light and no sense
of ultimate direction, you make one turn
then another and another and arrive
at the clearing from which the way is obvious.
My expectations of a longer work were based
on rooted wonders, buds and blossoms
crying to be plucked from a forest of memory
and arranged like ikebana with a balance and aesthetic,
so the themes would be displayed and all could follow.
These go even deeper than the fertile things of beauty
only you could make and honeysuckle so much pleasure
in our parents' prideful eyes. No, I'm referring
to our talents unfulfilled as well as realized,
co-starring in the cartoon of our lives with relatives,
the soap-opera of our parents' hopes for us -
which we know outran all hopes for themselves,
to births and deaths and far beyond to dying,
actually to all the moments and events
that we could name, and I am saying these
are wondrous, yes, and are the flora in our greenhouse,
and even more the binding joy and sorrow
of experience and observation shared in context
calling this one weed, that a volunteer,
and these bouquet and those disasters
unredeemed by any metaphor—all of this
is almost what I've come to value most.
The path that passes wonders
is the phone call in the night.
Your voice, your ear,
the fact that you are there,
the vast acreage canopied.

Wisdom

My bubbe hardly spoke and was considered
very wise. One socially demanding weekend
she did advise I could not be in two places
with one tuchas. And my father told me he remembered
when the witch from one floor up had stopped by twice
and the Friday challah didn't rise each time, my bubbe
warded off the woman's evil eyes by throwing her
the devil's horns with her right index finger
and pinky when her back was turned. When the challah
did rise, all agreed some heavy lessons had been learned.
Early on, some friends had warned me days would come
when I would fall in love with people for their youth alone.
They implied, I thought, I would be older when that happened.
Hah! Surprise, surprise. I have come to pride myself on
healthy skepticism and clear distinctions between correlations
and causality, evidence and anecdotes. I know myself
as one who shies from expectations based on notions
of a universe consistent over time and subject
to a uniformity of laws in different places.
I wonder whether bubbe held her tongue because she thought
that every kind of pride was sinful, even pride in knowledge,
and because of how words pass for wisdom to the young.

Visitor

American, Jew, father – when my dad counted those
on his fingers, I didn't realize he was listing the things
he was willing to die for. I made the connection later
when he pooh-poohed the problem of captives
deciding which family member to sacrifice
in purchase of the others' freedom. "I've had a life,"
he said, and added, "It could happen in this place, too;
here's a history lesson: we're just passing through.
People want to be rooted. Our people tried
and the ones who considered themselves German died.
Pray for prosperity. You won't be blamed for that."

For all the times I called on federal agencies
or went to meetings in government offices
this poem's title appeared in sans-serif capital letters
on tags I wore, reminding us all that those
who live here are the law and they like that,
these former school crossing guards, these
form-filers, aspiring "servant leaders,"
among them the loyal and the dedicated,
and all bureaucrats. They wear a different badge
than the field laborers and supplicants looking
for their lobbyists and wondering where the restrooms are.

Pull the focus high above the nation's capital
and you can see the waves of immigrants
beating at the borders, cleansing the coasts
then the inlands with tides of their blood,
tilling and seeding the fertile valleys,
making orchards big with apples, cherries, oranges.
That same flow that cleanses this country periodically
ran across the Bering Strait, across the big seas,

swells from the south over rivers and scrub lands,
desert and every terrain that scavengers rule,
runs in the veins of my sister and me; there is
no escaping the passages of which we all were a part.
The idea is: we're part of this flow and it's also within us,
leading to and away from the heart that is more than a metaphor.
When hits, hurts, abrasions and cuts of these travels
sink into, bruise below or show on the skin,
things thicken, bond, scab over. Healing isn't pretty.
My dad said you are always in transition.
Keep a bag packed. Try to make decisions.
Love means you know how to stay in contact.

Matilda Mark, Marine Park

> Eternity is in love with the productions of time.
> - William Blake

Overture

One way you can identify the great truths
is that their opposites are also in a big way true,
so you are forced to pursue your quest for guidance
by reliving anew the most persistent images you've accrued.
Poetry may be emotion recollected in tranquility
as Wordsworth suggests, but tranquil is a victory
which can come easily, or have to follow
recognition of a ripe symbolic moment
and the frantic race to capture an eternity
before some twitter floods a synapse
and all you ever could do after would be recollect.

* * *

My mother had grown smaller by this time
and the shock of overnight her jet hair
turning white had long since passed.
I see our silhouettes as from a distance.
Then, on new mown grass, I can see us standing
— it's Marine Park, we are perfectly encircled
by the mile-long bicycle track, beyond which
are the basketball courts within high wire fences,
cement walls for handball and stickball,
the bocci run, swings and symmetrical trees—
the sinking sun low in the sky behind us;
adjacent, the playground, the perilous parallel bars
and the fear of cement every child who fell there

still carries in scars and feels in the fresh pain
of skinned knees, abraded arms, young foreheads
bleeding and scraped (what could designers
of parks have been thinking?).

[We digress a moment to attend a meeting
of the Industry Standards Committee of the
National Association of Playground Designers and Builders.
"Imagine," says one, "the Next War
and the sad sinew of our soldiers to measure up
if we coddle them in youth.
Cement is the answer, gentlemen!"
"Wait," says another, "supposing we take little rocks
and disperse them throughout the cement?"
"Yes!" the committee says as one.
And the chairman, "When they graduate from the sandpit,
they enter the world of contention and pain;
they have mothers to prepare and protect them.
Let us not interfere in the order of nature and nations.
You are nodding; cement then, with little rocks, and by acclamation!"]

And then, I see we're standing close together
and my mother sports the gray wool cloche
with brightly colored sequins that she crocheted herself
and the light breeze from the bay beyond the park
is still for a moment. I can just catch the scent
of her sweet, floral perfume, White Shoulders,
and I know she would look up at me if she could,
but, bent and rounded now, she steadies herself
with a hand on my elbow, takes a step back,
and turns her whole body towards the playground,
where what I remember most clearly
is hanging suspended from the horizontal ladder,
the unforgiving pavement down below

three times my body's length, trying to swing
rung to rung in orangutan rhythm
to the vertical ladder at the other end.

My father always saw the humor
in my painful transitions, halfway
between his genuine, unselfish hopes for me
("I look forward to when you're the one who runs faster.")
and laughing out loud at my inadequacies.
But journeys for mother were serious things,
pathways through dangers. Her older sister, only seven,
coughed away her little life to Spanish flu—
so helpless, all of them, the parents, too.
Afterwards, my mother was the eldest,
and responsible for younger sisters, younger brother,
from which she, also, never would recover.

In fact, I have no memory of her laughing
even once. To my surprise, when the director
of my dissertation asked me why so late in life
I wanted that degree, and I replied
"This is my biggest uncompleted task and
time to let my mother know I'll never starve,"
and he said, "Why don't I just write your mother
that you've done it?" I, who'd hoped to be my father,
said, instead, "Let's just get serious."

There's a photo of a girl I never knew who's lying propped up
by her elbow on a towel in the sand at Coney Island,
coal black hair, curvaceous, not a hint of smile,
looks directly at you, mesmerizing, you would never
even think of pretty, only beautiful,
and self-possessed, there could be no decisions
made by others touching her that she would

tolerate without a judgment; there within
the depths of onyx eyes and framed
by lashes black and lush as a small meteor
might splash up from a pool of coal tar, you can see
the elemental strength of her opinions.

There is no way to summarize the complex passions of the woman
who instructed me that blood is thick compared to water,
who defended me from parents of the schoolmates I fought with,
from teachers' shattered expectations, all the clerics I disappointed,
any criticism, really, except hers. Her own mother,
she reminded me from time to time, arrived alone
from Hungary aged twelve and never saw again her parents,
yet she didn't speak to that same mother for eight years,
and none of us knew why, and she not telling,
was offended by her closest sister—another eight-year silence,
and then, her only brother, for his final twenty years,
never gave my father any explanations, but encouraged
the bewildered and potentially isolated—me and my sister—
to maintain with all these distanced kin good family relations.

It's a mixed blessing to be loved ferociously, to be
a vehicle for high aspirations thwarted by circumstances,
by choices vaguely understood, choices unrevealed,
to be warned and shielded from harm,
to be taught that little things are metaphors
for big things in art, but in life,
the little things really are big things as well.
You do grow skilled at how to be attentive
as excellent lovers and the best of serial killers
understand, which means, dear reader, you learn
that when someone else cares in that special way,
nothing you do, nothing you say, including attempts
to portray situations as funny, is actually a digression.

The downside of such an early love
is it can lead to expectations unattainable.
You can believe you really are important
as you have been treated
and you can feel guilty always
for your own incapability
to love with uncontrollable intensity.
But, to go through life and never be loved
by anyone in that way would be to be
the infinitely folded Samurai sword
asleep in its scabbard of tooled leather,
lying on a cushioned bed of silk
atop an ornate sideboard painted the color of verdigris—
the most highly evolved, potentially lethal
and quietist object in its universe,
dreaming about the hand of a brutal champion
to test its mettle to the point of breaking.

The aging of ferocity is not pretty,
neither in the ones we love nor in ourselves.
It doesn't lend itself to mellowing
like the wood of violins and cellos,
betrays instead, the odor of a perishable
meant to be consumed in ripe perfection.
All my mother's fears spread and engulfed her,
foreign people and their languages and businesses,
place of birth and neighborhoods unrecognizable,
schools home to guns and violence, America
adrift on the international scene, all the same time
as her physical decline, so much out of control
she stayed indoors and shrank the world to simple food
consumed in the spume of right-wing radio rants
and medicines so frequently required
that even rest in sleep was compromised.

Perhaps I could have learned
to be dispassionate, the lesson of the Gita:
judge those tied to you by family or love
as if they were a stranger,
by their righteousness alone.
I think I could have learned that had my mother
had an easier departure, had she been spared
indignity, the gift of all those sullen so-called nurses,
and the final loss of privacy.
But, even to the end, my sister and I
arrived as to a coronation
in the little barricaded space, a realm,
although besieged by pain and chaos,
where what we did and thought
meant something.

And all of this is why the vision of my mom and me
I try to keep is outdoors in the golden hour sun of Marine Park
where the strength of her aroma is sufficient arsenal
to hold at bay the sharpness of recently cut fescue,
the city sewage flowing underneath the nearby grate,
the sea air carrying inland its salty scent of jelly, weed
and mollusk, simple life forms tossed up on the sand.
In all the transient world this place is where my mother's will
to clear and guide us down a providential path is still inviolable,
and here my mother takes my hand without a word
and turns to lead me safely in the long walk home.

* * *

Coda

When you write a poem, you create occasions,
put in some ideas, opinions, and the like,
give it shape, direction and you really cannot
do much more, or there is nothing left the poem
can imply; to live, it needs its own soul
and its own ability to surprise. Ultimately,
that is the way my mother treated me, and
not because she thought some things
were better left to chance; because, reluctantly,
she had to put up with the dates, companions,
and an unknown spouse to whom I opened up
the family, my move away, my godless house,
my jobs in new professions lacking history,
my plantless, petless, childless abode,
the puzzling, disappointing news of my divorce—
all beyond her comprehension—and still she
would defend me—she, and only she
could be my critic and interrogator;
even as the circle of her tolerance narrowed,
so tightened as a seasoned wedding band her loyalty.
I admit it took all that, and the not entirely
free pass from the hard, judgmental parts of me
she authored, to force me to love her.

Sailing to Los Angeles

When I was a child in Brooklyn,
the encyclopedia you bought in the grocery store
one volume each month for a year
lived on a bookcase shelf within arm's reach of my bed
and when you got to Yap you saw an engraving
of a brown boy my age wearing only a thu
loin cloth draped around, front and back,
standing next to an oval, six-foot high stone
with a hole in its middle, the traditional coin of the realm.
That boy was a brother to me. I saw us go,
once each year, with our Yapese father, we called it
on bivouac, beyond the neighboring island, Ulithi,
to an unpeopled place we gave the name Guy Laang – "to see sky."
We packed dried meat and fruit and water.
We walked out of our house on Yap, past the palm tree against which
a big stone coin leaned where my father always said that's the one
that will buy you a wife. And I always thought yes a nice big one.
We took the ferry to Ulithi,
then canoed for three hours to Guy Laang.

We carried all we needed including the two folding tents.
We camped two weeks completely isolated
to do nothing and everything. It was the mild season.
We took a flashlight for the purpose of not using it.
We had the moon and the stars.
On the little hill at the center of this world,
trees gave us shelter. Through them
in every direction we watched the water.
We memorized the currents to paddle on, to float in.

One evening on the sandy beach,
my Yapese father asked me what I saw.

I said what the flying frigate bird sees.
He asked me what I heard.
I said I heard the wind and the fish swimming,
the ones that glide, the ones that slice the water,
the schools that turn in unison.
My father said you mean you see them.
And I realized that he had forgotten.
And that meant that even I could forget.
He told me his father sailed to Los Angeles
a long time ago. The name of that city sang in my ear.
I determined to visit that far off place.
I thirsted to learn what the angels who live there remember.

The Literary Party

> O my Luve's like a red, red rose
> That's newly sprung in June
> — Robert Burns

Let's send a little love to the scientists
for that portion of their mission that makes them
work so diligently to prove what everyone already knows,
that once you are moving along, it takes a special effort
to slow down, that if you pay close attention, you can
pretty much quantify anything, even how things
attract each other, and if you pay really, really
close attention, you are better served by metaphor,
and along with this love – and gratitude – each of us
should share an image illustrating, dramatizing, we
could say exhibiting, a revelation scientists could work on
forever to prove. For instance, it's a good hypothesis
that pain and pleasure have the same pop at a deep level,
which gets interpreted in many complex ways for what
the pop means–fight or flight, feeling, insight–kind
of like the way all colors of the human skin are densities
of a single pigment. And one of the reasons we are better
served by metaphors is that we know they always break
on down to the next level, where we have to look more closely;
love, if like a rose, what are its thorns, if so like music,
why does it not dissipate in air, if I am just as deep within it
as my love is fair, what happens as our spring and summer pass;
rejoice, you scientists and poets, you will always find employment
in the half-life of a metaphor. There is a room
inhabited by the literary world and in that half-light
Rita Dove embraces St. James Infirmary Blues,
Bob Lynch's fingers dance among piano keys,
I'm counterpoint on washtub bass,

and who could have imagined how the Poet Laureate could sing
that song so full of pain? The room is like that high abode
celestial resonant with all the desperate prayers flying up and in
and all the answers swirling in a vortex, some miraculous
connections will occur and some just as miraculously
won't, laws begging for description operate here
relentlessly as in the rest of nature; sadly, happiness alone,
as any scientist or artist, even clergy, might observe, does not result
in what it feels like to play within this metaphor for heaven.

Seals Sunning on the Ice

When we prepared to travel back in time
we were surprised to find how sad unraveling hope would be
undoing strand by strand the tightly woven fabric of possibility
in all directions. Accordingly we balanced this with celebration
by the friends and much recounting of the youth and promise
much of it fulfilled and marriage children the divorce
how many loved this traveler and were loved
some awkward humor here both wry and tearful smiles
and the son plays his guitar the daughter recites her poem
and then the friends recount the lost one's visions
toward the end imaginary journeys to a lighthouse
and requests for notes with reminiscences we all sent them
they were read aloud our paths all crossing in the air.

When I go through my photos of the conference
that marked the boundary of the final healthy days
I find the image of us standing close together
on the deck of the tour boat in front of the glacier
that calved a minute later with a crack like a gunshot
surrounded by berglets or berglitos or berglinos
what difference do these words make while
the seals sunning nearby on their slivers of floating ice
were fat and shiny with enough metaphor to last a lifetime.

It surely is a blessing when the seals are only seals
and your breath in the air before you
is your breath in the air before you
when what you feel is arms around each other's shoulders
and you look into the iris of the camera
as you pour into and stack up in the multimillion pixel grid
and you are smiling just before the flash
so that becomes the organizing principle of this
specific slice this universe particular and forever
the seals sunning on the ice.

Cobblers

In Hungary, more than a hundred years ago
my great grandfather was a shoemaker
and he lived like a trapper in Idaho:
months for making, months for traveling, selling.
He must have dreamed of dwelling in one village
year-round, people coming to his house
to make their purchase. Which could never be.
When would people ever value shoes that way?
Would it take a special pain, a new level of duress?
But what could be of more importance
than imagining the shoe
that's worth a voyage to possess?

Think about the pair he made himself
to wear for half a year of pulling a cart
over what a road was then. He must have loved
every part that made his feet feel they could manage
where he was and get him through it all,
not wear out sole or heel, and walk him home.

Making each shoe individually
with his own hands from the toughest hides,
he must have felt the same
about the shoes he made to sell.
This was mine. Now it's yours. Use it well.

Where quality resides is difficult to say;
materials, how pieces fit together,
care for people we will never know
have parts to play, but in the end
it's not that difficult to tell the way
a work of art, a shoe, a city has been made.

Sometimes with objects made from clay
or leather, visions out of air, the great work
is declaring they're not good enough:
this product is not done; it's still in process;
that one we thought was finished is still rough,
move hell or heaven, its making might outlive us.

So, high among important tasks at hand
for starting off today or any day
is to remind ourselves we understand
our city is a poem—and what poetry
has to sell may not be new,
but must be constantly invented anyway.
Whatever life we cobble
will have its story to tell.
This was mine. Now it's yours. Use it well.

Journeyman

I placed a jar in Tennessee,
And round it was, upon a hill.
It made the slovenly wilderness
Surround that hill.

- Wallace Stevens

Divine

sometimes you get a line
from out of nowhere and you think
this must be gotten from a holy ghost

except that you are so far from
belief that you are almost hostile
to the meaning that a deity brings

a circuit firing randomly
a lightning strike into
the blighted stand of birch trees

divine is nothing you are
constituted to admit incontinence
alone suffices to dispute it

and yet you have this gift
that makes you cold in the night
because you have to toss the blanket

and get up turn on the light reach for
find the pen and write it down
fellow traveler in the dark I am

afraid it's only you who understands divinity
as the earnest courtesan receiving me,
who shows up random as a line

of poetry, and now above all irony
must get it up herself ignite and make
something in the shape of love

The Best Part

of being an English teacher,
said my seventh grade mentor, Mr. Rodman,
impossibly sleek and feline in his blazer,
button-down shirt and rep tie,
was being the one at the Friday night party
who said the cleverest thing,
the thing that someone still remembered
on a bleak Monday morning
when the bell would ring.

Bananas

Have you ever noticed how few references
to bananas there are in the English language
before 1600? I have. And I can tell you
there are other fruits galore. Shakespeare
in all his horticultural profusion never wrote
the word banana in a play–a lemon, yes,
oranges, too, since they mimic the color
of a jealous complexion, and they do rot,
sir, as virtue tainted by sinful behavior.
Nor would a Tudor kitchen smell so bountiful
devoid of dates and quinces in its pastry.
And that, my boon companions, is why
monkeys, chimpanzees particularly,
will never type a Shakespeare play
no matter how many or how long the days
they work once they have peeled a banana skin.
It is, for prospective Shakespearean monkeys,
the forbidden fruit, its taste the unpardonable sin.

I will assemble a band of monkey brothers –
and sisters – we have workforce advantages now
that Shakespeare and his ilk did not,
who have neither seen nor heard tell
of bananas, and they will demonstrate
the true potential of imagination free
of learned desires, free of images
inspired externally, they will randomly
illuminate the caves of the innate,
so, from the primitive primate,
perhaps we, higher on the evolutionary tree

can extrapolate, glimpse–yea shape, our powers to be.

As any good scientist or program evaluator
will affirm, an intervention may result in an outcome
more desirable than that intended, otherwise
we would not have those yellow sticky tabs
originally meant to bond forever and Viagra
would be a third-rate choice for ailments of the cardiac
rather than numero uno for the amiable kind.

Even so, I was wildly surprised on one morning to find
my monkeys had written a couple of lines
not of Shakespeare, but Blake:

Ah, sunflower, weary of time
Who countest the steps of the sun, seeking
banana, banana, banana, banana, banana
then gibberish until the breakfast feeding.
I key entered back: when you write banana,
a thing you have never, what are you imagining?
They wrote: we will key enter no longer
a long time ago we left words because
they did not work for us media rule
maybe for you write your own story yours
is the kingdom the power banana banana banana
banana banana banana banana banana banana
and ever since grimaces, big grins and gibberish

Drinking and Driving

When I hear "Don't drink and drive"
I remember holding on for dear life
in the passenger seat when the drunkest friend
I ever needed pressed the pedal to the floor
and the other time an academic buddy high on speed
flew us up the thruway to New England for a weekend
at a hundred and ten and how incredibly
competent they were inhabiting the same
Dionysian lust and how desperately delusional
I was believing they were *so* good at this
because they did these young things often
instead of how much better everything would be
if they did such things while sober or
how much more likely to keep breathing
we would be if *never* were when things like this were done.
A gust of wind, a little patch of ice,
those are two out of a thousand authors
that would have written articles with words like
"mangled," "inexplicable," and "are survived by grieving."
Now in front of you could be a shopping flyer
or a takeout menu for a local restaurant
or a really good poem by somebody else.
There's no denying the attraction of fantasy pasts
with risks that worked or might not have, the tease
of alternative futures based on different choices.
Different, doesn't even have to be much better, sounds like fun.
The drunk may hit the high notes or be a sloppy singer,
but who can write a better drinking song
than that would-be drinker, sober as a toad in mud,
sitting alone in a dim-lit, over-heated room,
yearning for a brimming glass,
a steering wheel and the open road?

The Topic of All Poems

All poems are about love, or beauty,
or the singularity of people and things
in the eyes of God, or, paradoxically,
the commonality of the poet with what
the poet sees, until the black beetle
on the wall reveals the lie, the opposite
of empathy is what you feel, that otherness
is equally a quality that defines us;
separation from the holy crawls around
the moist and darker places. Transfixed
in light, that is what reflectively illuminates
the topic of all poems, that hard carapace,
the rainbow splayed upon its shiny surface,
the juice within that we imagine,
the thought we're living in the age of insects
and the image of it cracked and crushed;
assessing now our distance and identity,
we ask are we less creepy omnivores
because we have an eye for poetry?

Moxibustion

"In the beginning was the Word…."
John 1:1

"Mommy" and "Daddy" are among the first
and they are welcomed with applause and celebration
as if no child ever said anything like that before.
Then begin so many to arrive, so quickly and so numerous,
they aren't even noticed and methodically accrue.

Yet on occasion one shows up
an unexpected stranger at your threshold
or perhaps the carnival has come to town
or you have wandered into a bodega,
pet store full of perched and pacing animal exotica,
or unfamiliar accidental bandwidth on a new device.

Or it can happen we trip over some old noun,
a battered basket sitting there forever
off to one side on the door step,
that reveals the coiled snake of new surprises.
It's as if a suit of clothes we've seen on many people
is inhabited by someone we don't recognize
but who turns out to be a kindred spirit
worthy of knowing beyond the smile, behind the eyes.

However you encounter moxibustion,
it denotes the burning of the Chinese mugwort,
which is *artemisia argyi*, near the skin, and it can be the smoky
or the smoke-free variety, or in a charcoal stick-like form.
Where? At acupuncture point UB67. That's right.

Where's that? It's at the lower outside point just under
each of the nails of your littlest toes. That's right. Why?
To re-position breech births – when the baby's bottom
wants out first – and you need a somersault inside
so the head will crown instead. That's right.
For 10 to 15 minutes ten days in a row. Yes.
Because the smoldered mugwort warmth for many
thousand moons has risen from the littlest toenails
of mommies in China along an invisible pathway,
pipeline, a silk road of energy turning the downside
up right side down. Here is the word used in a sentence:
You have been sentenced to a lifetime contemplating moxibustion.
This is the word, I mean the world, in which you live.

Chambers

1. The apse above the altar tops the reach
   rounds off this little universe
   may illustrate the starry heavens
   flights of angels hovering there
   The chancel to the East
   may embrace a choir
   or vestry where the pious could prepare

2. The bird's high volume heart has four
   proportionally large compared to mammal
   beat five times within a second
   to propel the hollow bones and feathers
   through the vanquished atmosphere
   The same rapidity would explode another
   species and the sudden load come crashing

3. Bullets are a tight fit within theirs
   The emptying of several all at once
   is full of sexuality each missile thrusting
   towards its barrel like the roulette ball
   whose carouseling slot lies yearning
   for its jumpy soul to come to rest within
   and open up a tomb of consequences

4. There are so many ways the memory
   of your voice fills drives and penetrates
   the rooms I wander to escape devotion
   I am dizzy with each caught and carried breath

5. On the surface of our faces now
   my index finger traces
   to those little indentations
   just beneath our noses just above
   the destination where our lips touch
   echoes emanating then from unexpected places

Lucy Aloft

Lucy has been at the centre of a vigorous debate about the role, if any, of arboreal locomotion in early human evolution. It is therefore ironic that her death can be attributed to injuries resulting from a fall, probably out of a tall tree, thus offering unusual evidence for the presence of arborealism in this species.

From an abstract of *Nature*, Kappelman et al, 8/29/2016

We weren't there, so don't really know
what she was doing up in a tree – hypothetically up
40 feet to cause the bone damage revealed recently,
diminutive Australopithecus having left behind
the grasping toes in trade for the sleek flatter models
better suited to locomote over the open savanna.

We imagine her high on a limb
above the reach of predators, perhaps in a
jerry-rigged perch, perhaps with a mate
or season's companion, we can't say for sure
how secure the little hominin felt just before
her mortal moment, but she was on celebrity tour
from Ethiopia where she landed to Houston
for a show then to Austin for the x-ray
displaying the "greenstick" fractures, the kind
that happen when you are alive but never heal,
suggesting our ancestor's "vertical deceleration event"
marked the sudden last breath that she ever spent.

And still she occupies a special place, her
flexible thumbs angling halfway across her palms,
fully committed to walking along upright now
on her trend-setting arched metatarsals,
learning to signal with gestures and sounds,

her surrounding family soon to be migrating,
subjugating every other species
but rodents and insects for the rest of time.
Absent all the images a world developing had yet to spawn,
there must have been edible and aromatic things
along the high branches one could feel crawling,
smell budding and leafing. Three million years ago
the impulse to climb had to be irresistible,
so much to explore and more terrain to be observed
from where a shrike or fly-catcher could sit
than one curious little monkey-girl could capture in a lifetime.

The World as Garden

Yes, that was my big idea –
because I'm not aware of many people
plowing through an introduction
of a vintage more recent than
The Preface to the Lyrical Ballads–
to set a couple of observations
daffodil-bulb-like
in the soil of the text; for instance,
that each of these poems,
and probably everyone else's, too,
is part about something particular,
but all about poetry itself as well,
the premise of each:
that life needs meaning;
so then, though it might be said
that his lines could be, um,
labored on occasion, or, um,
a little preachy, still,
an anthologist like you might decide
he (meaning me) was clever enough to be
companionable, at least
in one's leisure time, of which,
his other plotted point was,
there really isn't any.

Finally

> It is now understood that gut microbiota collectively contain
> 3.3 million genes, a hundred times the number of human genes.
>
> - Susan Scutti, "A Gut Reaction," *Newsweek*, 11/29/2013

We don't know whether to call the weakness
betrayed by your pathetic ritual of coffins
ignorance or arrogance.

And who are you anyway,
you fragile coalition of the momentarily self-conscious,
you illusionistas of individuality and community?

We precede you, we accompany your pathetic notions
of birth, growth and finality, and we outlast you.
Oh, we used the word "pathetic" more than once?
Well, what does that tell you?
Please don't mistake our derision for anger;
we like having you for our fashion industry.

We know the purpose of the gods you invent
is to deny us our dignity.
No wonder it took so long for you
to realize your upsets, doubts and inspirations
are crowd sourced, flash mobs of ours, and not
among the shiny or the shattered shards of self-reflection
that you like to praise or blame for everything
because it makes you feel important.

Anyhoo, now we have decided to show up
and we'd like some gratitude for what we do.
You could begin by thanking us,
the hundred trillion (that's right, *trillion*) strong

whose odor you decided not to like,
whose functions you decided are the meaning of disgust,
whom you treat just as badly as the throng of lower classes
of the other biomasses your exalted thoughtfulness
supposedly disposes you to treat with empathy,
yes, by thanking us, for everything we process
that is really you, and for the history of poetry
you have been claiming for the few, the perfumed,
the so-called conscious, all along.

Journeyman

Poetry is, after all, that craft of the journeyman
who shows up and does one task today,
another tomorrow; who plants the flag atop
the hill under fire from the evil adversary;
who submerges and sprays torpedoes in all directions;
who takes one drink too many and maims innocent civilians;
who surprises everyone by sending the family home
and, boasting the bright red headband of the enemy,
pilots like a flaming pie the plane of some didactic protest
into the window-eyed face of the skyscraper;
who, ultimately, betrays every constituency,
kisses your daughter farewell inappropriately,
and moves on; whom you remember times you liked,
times you didn't. Trouble is, some damned thing
always needs fixing: fixing like you fix
a faucet, fixing like you fix a dog.
This journeyman keeps a journal
with your real name in it,
next to the pet ones you like to be called.

Throwing out the Poems

Congratulations on your tentative decision
to rip up the poems of your youth.
You can never cheat death
by publishing your juvenilia.
No, you can't cheat death like that,
or, as my not-for-profit organization
friends would say, you would not
be cheating death in a *sustainable* way,
because your eternal debris,
like the frozen junk, parts of a thousand
failed space probes, little orbiting worlds
without end, would be so ridiculous
flitting around the faces and ears
of the ones you hoped to impress
with your precociousness that
you would out-sing Keats's nightingale
for the sweet opportunity to die.

You have to beat death on its own terms
like the reluctant, corruptible,
disintegrating, vindictive,
jealous lover of your own body
that you are, willing to do
whatever it takes, anything at all,
that will implant your sinewy sentences
in the warm and wondrous breath
of a stranger, as even your beloved becomes
when all the shining objects of time stop swinging,
and you realize a voice is saying
"wake up, you can wake up now,"

but you are not done dreaming.

And still you hate to shred those early poems
although you do own how embarrassing
the lyric sequence of your needs and hopes is,
what a shame it is that from the ardent naivete
of young ambition and imagined future wisdom
and awe of nature's pregnant beauty, you
and most of humankind have not created even OK art,
that every flesh-like bud and blossom has to wither first,

though those irritating particles of your earliest discovered self
regenerated every morning in the corners of your eyes
for all these years have served their sticky purpose,
which no other person's compliments prevented or dissolved,
and you will count your wintry dignity a kind of victory
if only you can keep aglow the smoldering ember of the secret
that, all your trophied triumphs notwithstanding,
you are only now awakening and you are not,
not yet, done dreaming.

Cicadas

foot prints
tire tracks
jet trails
spider threads strung in trees
ashes
dreams
shooting stars
charts of how diseases spread
breaths like frosted breezes

with all the animate and the fossil pathways
latticing our lives, you have to wonder
what's the difference,
what's the source of death's pride
and where does that reside.

While cicada sounds rasp around my ears
like top-volume-distorted music of the spheres
I'm looking at the insect husks
as symbols of all shed affairs
and thinking of the past implied.
Just hours ago, these were the salmon
of the ground, skin burning off with lust
and friction, every millimeter loosened
like a flaking scale, a token of delusion,
evidence desire is how we trick ourselves
into another generation, the arabesque of flesh
with flesh igniting young assassins who replace us
after turning us grotesque

and yet we understand that every drop of rain
surrounds a speck of unique dust:
the opposite of a rum cordial,
yes, very like the planet floating
in its sea of atmosphere.

I met the curator of buildings and the grounds
of Canterbury Village in New Hampshire.
When she went out from Winterthur
she'd learned affection for the lore
of drainage, landscaping, how to "exclude"
a house from mice and bats and weather;
an engineering firm was paying well for her
to site, comply and such, but not to value
or interpret or preserve the story, the terrain
and what was built. So, since the tasks
most near her heart were those that planned
and plumbed by giving to a place
the voice of what was done there most worth telling,
her most compelling choice was taking off for Shaker town.
She left the job that had become for her
a shell of real work, a glove that didn't fit her hand.

In its dense, encrusted shell, the hermit crab
seems better suited than humankind
to contemplate perfection; ever vulnerable,
finally, we peel off our uniforms,
fly to each other exposed, like those
who left these exoskeletons behind.
Remember Ezra Pound, fascist and going crazy,
railing against "usura," and saying
insuring the sea ships had spent the creativity
civilization was supposed to mine?

It's not a stupid thought that high deeds
come from risk without a net, or that
the underside of excess profit is another's debt;
that's why I'll never buy he went so mad
as destitute of empathy and lost.
A family and charity don't seem first rank needs
when plankton are your sage and school;
further up the food chain, kinship gets you linked
to others with their doomed and blessed desires;
freedom from them then comes at greater cost.

So I will try to find a pattern
in the scattered, empty carapaces drying
on the walk, strewn along the lawn, the driveway,
fallen on the porch and on the steps, and,
vestige of the mortal struggle to emerge,
clinging all around the house
to window screens—like words to pages.
Has the will to live escaped them, moved along? Or
is that will made stronger framed in desiccated metaphor,
abstract mementos mori, from which courage
comes to ask: where is their meaning,
what is that music throbbing from the woods,
from leaves and branches hanging in the way
of all that climbs and flies in unseen places,
rises up in rhythm like the choir to the stage,
and leans in to circle and to serenade those brittle
artifacts of passion yesterday until
every blood-filled fool alive attests
that poetry abides in emptiness.

Author's Notes

These author's notes take advantage of a special opportunity to provide some context, share an observation, emphasize a point, or enhance a reference. Ambiguity is sometimes intended and sometimes serendipitous, but almost always, from my perspective, welcome, so I hope anything I write in a note is not received by a reader as limiting any of the interpretations possible to apply to the words of a poem on its page.
— JK

p. 10, Envy of Robert Hass's Poem
Listeners and readers have been entertained by Odysseus' means of survival for thousands of years. I love Hass's reconstruction of the sirens episode around the complex power of interacting imaginations. In the Homeric narrative, I'm taken with how Odysseus becomes a hero even though he has no super powers, the fast-changing scenarios in his world cannot be managed by preparation, and his foes have special – even magical – capacities as well as experience greater than his. This sensual thrill-seeker knows enough to stuff his crew's ears but is compelled to hear the deadly sirens sing himself. His tactics of cunning, deceit, disguise, emotional manipulation, cold calculation, mercilessness and desperate risk-taking enable him to survive in spite of his flaws in this most modern of ancient epics.

p. 13, Defining Irony
To mark the 50th anniversary of Sylvia Plath's death by suicide *The Guardian* ran an article in which prominent women described what the author meant to them. Multi-talented Lena Dunham asked her Twitter followers what they thought and one wrote about *The Bell Jar*, 'it made me feel less alone.' If only the book had done that for its author.

p. 17, Stichomancy
I encourage the reader to try this, either alone or with others (which I find to be very different experiences). That I found Banach space this way is true, and I decided to stick with and push that event to see where

its poem led. My advice is to think of a question, problem, decision, etc., and then open a book. You won't need a prompt if you are alone; if with others, each player can articulate an issue, then the payoff is hearing people's different interpretations of how the stichomantic word or phrase or sentence or section of writing relates or instructs or judges or predicts. It might also be interesting to compare the results from using more than one book – say, a book of poems, a science text, an encyclopedia, a cheap romance.

p. 27, Blake epigraph
In Blake's prophetic myth, *The Four Zoas*, the figure of Los represents the human faculty that provides form and shape, enabling forces and issues to be engaged meaningfully. Los builds Golgonooza, which can be thought of as a kind of space-time continuum where all artistic engagement takes place and lives. In his brilliant study, *Fearful Symmetry*, critic Northrup Frye illuminates this topic.

p. 29, Affluence
Several different stories have been attached over millennia to the persona of an over-confident Phrygian monarch. In one, Midas rashly expresses his preference for the music of the faun Pan over the music of Apollo. The insulted god changes his ears into the ears of an ass. In another, Midas is offered any wish in reward for a favor he had done the god Dionysus, who cautions him to think carefully. Midas rashly asks that whatever he touches be turned to gold, only to have his beloved daughter run into his arms and be transformed into a statue. Though these Midas stories are of separate origin, they reinforce the mythic message–to a ruler and to a people–that a character flaw can undermine power and prosperity.

p. 32, Part
This is one of what I call "dictionary poems." The challenge is to identify a word that has several seemingly unrelated meanings, then to enable a coherence for those meanings to emerge in a poem without using that word, except as the title. So with "part" one can work to relate what the

Red Sea is fabled to have done, a separation, a piece of a whole, a feature of combed hair, a role in a play, etc. See also "Chambers" and "Visitor."

p. 33, The Art of War
In his 1962 novel, *Island*, Aldous Huxley describes an isolated utopian society (most notably, its education system) increasingly threatened by its surrounding dystopian world. In paradisiacal Pala, as part of a pervasive inculcation of interconnection between people and with the environment, the parrots are taught to caw "Attention." The reference to IEDs (improvised explosive devices) is a reminder that the radical psychology of war in the name of a cause can seem to justify directing violence at active opponents as well as those who are uncommitted to a conflict and might not even be aware of it. Raised also is the very challenging issue area of what consideration, culpability or risk is deserved by one who is unengaged in (and perhaps even ignorant of) the resolution of various kinds of inequity or conflict.

p. 37, Attractive Nuisance
The "attractive nuisance doctrine" attaches liability to something, such as a swimming pool, that is not illegal itself, but nevertheless represents a danger. (Like certain professions that exploit the power of language?) Suspensions of *habeas corpus* include Lincoln's detention of war prisoners and the internment of Japanese Americans during WW II. *Duces tecum* refers to the power of courts to order that materials or evidence be presented.

p. 39, Feeling Free
The words in quotation marks came from Donald J. Trump prior to his election as president of the United States.

p. 42, The M-Word
The author intentionally offers a reader or reciter the choice of the two-syllable "M-Word" or its four-syllable referent.

p. 45, Haeckel and cummings epigraphs
One of the mysteries that poems dramatize is how our most meaningful relationships with others shape us. In some instances, we seem to become like our influencers, in others we respond by becoming different, in still others a combination of responses can be observed, and then there are effects for which the cause remains mysterious. Consequently, the introductory quotations each contain truth and are contrary.

p. 47, Objects in Motion
The papers describing this monumental observation were published in 1965 and received the Nobel Prize in 1978. Basically, physicists noticed that wherever they pointed their telescope they observed background radiation for which only one theory provided them satisfaction. The artist and the scientist within each of us should continually ask each other, "So what?"

p. 49, The Penny
I wrote this poem after sharing a cab from an airport to a conference hotel with a woman I overheard asking the cab driver to take her to the hotel that was also my destination. Didn't take long to make up the part about the Greeks believing coins have souls and to borrow some content from the conversation we had in the cab. Elated, I called the woman and left a message offering to deliver a copy of the poem, but she never called back. I envision her telling her friends of her escape from an "*airport-cab poem-writing stalker.*"

p. 63, The Literary Party
For me, the literal details and transitory aspects of Burns' rose and melody love-metaphors undercut the dependability of his promise to love "till a' the seas gang dry." But maybe not. Please note that, in addition to her many recorded readings, the singing of Rita Dove can be enjoyed on several YouTube videos.

p. 65, Seals Sunning on the Ice
This poem is inspired by Dan Harpole, whose professional life was dedicated to public service and integrating artistic experience in community life. He chaired the Washington State Arts Commission, directed the Idaho Commission on the Arts, and was one of the elected presidents of the National Assembly of State Arts Agencies (NASAA) whom I partnered with as CEO. Our last conference together was in Anchorage.

p. 79, Chambers
A "dictionary poem." See "Part."

p. 81, Lucy Aloft
Training in the arts and humanities can enhance scientific inquiry and observation. It only requires a little imagination and empathy to consider that, even after a hominid's feet had evolved in favor of upright walking, there would still be motivations strong enough to make climbing a tree seem worth the effort.

p. 83, The World as Garden
The preface referred to is Wordsworth's manifesto (1800) for the meaning and value of what is now considered British "romantic" poetry.

p. 89, Cicadas
I have debated back and forth over years whether or not to delete the Ezra Pound section of this poem, understanding that both its allusiveness and logic are demanding of a reader. It stays in because, in the poem's litany of husks, what happens (to artists, scholars, decision makers and those who bear the consequences) when a discipline of the humanities is studied and applied without a motivational core of loving-kindness deserves a place.

C&R PRESS TITLES

NONFICTION

Women in the Literary Landscape by Doris Weatherford, et al
Credo: An Anthology of Manifestos & Sourcebook for Creative
Writing by Rita Banerjee and Diana Norma Szokolyai

FICTION

Last Tower to Heaven by Jacob Paul
No Good, Very Bad Asian by Lelund Cheuk
Surrendering Appomattox by Jacob M. Appel
Made by Mary by Laura Catherine Brown
Ivy vs. Dogg by Brian Leung
While You Were Gone by Sybil Baker
Cloud Diary by Steve Mitchell
Spectrum by Martin Ott
That Man in Our Lives by Xu Xi

SHORT FICTION
Notes From the Mother Tongue by An Tran
The Protester Has Been Released by Janet Sarbanes

ESSAY AND CREATIVE NONFICTION
In the Room of Persistent Sorry by Kristina Marie Darling
the Internet is for real by Chris Campanioni
Immigration Essays by Sybil Baker
Je suis l'autre: Essays and Interrogations
by Kristina Marie Darling
Death of Art by Chris Campanioni

POETRY
A Family Is a House by Dustin Pearson
The Miracles by Amy Lemmon
Banjo's Inside Coyote by Kelli Allen
Objects in Motion by Jonathan Katz
My Stunt Double by Travis Denton
Lessons in Camoflauge by Martin Ott
Millennial Roost by Dustin Pearson
Dark Horse by Kristina Marie Darling
All My Heroes are Broke by Ariel Francisco
Holdfast by Christian Anton Gerard
Ex Domestica by E.G. Cunningham
Like Lesser Gods by Bruce McEver
Notes from the Negro Side of the Moon by Earl Braggs
Imagine Not Drowning by Kelli Allen
Notes to the Beloved by Michelle Bitting
Free Boat: Collected Lies and Love Poems by John Reed
Les Fauves by Barbara Crooker
Tall as You are Tall Between Them by Annie Christain
The Couple Who Fell to Earth by Michelle Bitting